THE MORNING MELODY

SARBAJIT ROY

Contents

Contents

Contents

1. The Morning Melody

I woke to the sound of the morning bird's call,
A melody so sweet, a joy the heart did enthrall,
Music flowed through the air in elegant song,
Other birds joined in chorus and each sang along,
The leaves rustled in harmony, the breeze sublime notes brought,
Bees hummed in ecstasy, filled with happiness they had sought,
Life danced to the music as did the rays of the morning sun,
The day, garbed in colors to the tune of the music, had begun,
Every day on the earth shall wake with a lovely dream,
Showered in freedom's symphony,
life shall resplendent seem.

2. The Horizon

I walked towards the horizon, as it moved further away ,
Its limits unbounded, over vast realms it held sway,
Beyond lay the land of dreams, heaven's abode,
Where the red sun in its descent soothingly strode,
The hills in majestic silence beckoned as the breeze
Blew in caressing flow, rustling every leaf with fondful ease ,
Clouds sailed in grandeur, yet the horizon remained further beyond ,
Leading them to infinite realms, where dreams would respond,
Fleeting time, beyond life's vision before life's hopes does float ,
The mind pursues the enchanted path to the dreams towards the horizon so remote.

3. The Shores of the Ocean

On the shores of the ocean I walked, Amid the footsteps
of many, whose Footprints remained , till the waves Washed
them and returned ,
Only to arrive again
And wash many more,
As it had from ages ago
And from time immemorial;
With every wave I heard voices
Of the present and the past
As memories floating in the mind,
The vast ocean bowed to the earth
Every moment the waves touched Its hallowed shores and
Rolled quietly in obeisance;
Ages from now, they shall repeat
The same gestures, in a cycle
Perennial and eternal ,
On the sands of time.

4. Fallen Leaves

Fallen leaves
Everywhere,
The wind
Carries them away,
Sweeping away life;
New buds bloom
In abandon,
New leaves grow
With
Youthful vigor ;
A fresh breeze
Blows,
Leaves rustle ,
Whispering
To each other;
Only memories
Remain,
The sky knows
And the stream
That flows
To the river

And then
To the Ocean
Of Truth.

5. The Cricket's Song

When the sun has dipped from the horizon below
And to the earth the heavens do darkness bring,
The moon appears, in silvery lustrous glow
And the crickets together in chorus sing ;
Music fills the the ears of the child ,
In notes and rhythms all night long ,
From every bush and thicket in the wild
Bursts the cricket's vernal song ;
The stars pause in their motions to hear,
The moon smiles with joyous light,
The street dog listens with a strained ear,
Fireflies glow endlessly to the cricket's delight;
The child sleeps with a dream and smile
As the crickets chirp their lullaby along,
Fireflies and the night whisper all the while,
The river flows in symphony to the Cricket's eternal song .

6. The Dawn

Every minute and hour, the passing night
Welcomes the Dawn's soulful and golden light,
Humankind's dreams and hopes before the morn
Aspire for the first rays of the sun in the early Dawn ,
On the trees , the birds in concert their songs begin
As the golden fingers of sunlight with light fill the scene,
Darkness surrenders to the Divine image in eager zest,
The sun, rising as a canopy of gold, bids the stars to take their
nightly rest ,
The spreading rays of the sun shine softly on the city streets ,
The flurry of activity shall soon increase as every walker the
other greets ,
The beautiful moment brings freshness to the earth, the green
leaves and grass does it adorn,
The child with sleepy eyes wakes up to the new day , ushered
by the Divine Dawn.

7. The Rain

Rapturous winds blow
The clouds insane,
Streaks of forked lightning
Appear before peals
Of roaring thunder ,
The rain falls
In torrents of melody
On the murmuring stream
And the green grass,
Water collects and flows
With fluid mirth
As darkness shrouds
The afternoon sun ,
Watching the rainy shades,
Leaves , drenched with water
Sway with the wind ,
The intricacy and beauty
Of life
Is evident as
One loses oneself
In a world of lost smiles .

8. The Ocean

The vast expanse of acetylene blue
Meets the sky with reflected hue,
Below the reigning infinite calm ,
Lie profound depths of heaven's embalm;
On the far horizon bathed in radiant light,
Golden waves dance in sheer delight,
The murmuring waters do the sky beguile,
Singing their song in symphony every while;
With every undulating wave travels a dream,
Rising and ebbing with hopes that fulfilling seem ,
Humankind for ages has traveled the ocean's demesne ,
With the waves, history flows to the future as the past does
remain .

9. The Butterfly

With colored wings of fantasy , from flower to flower ,
The butterfly sails with sublime ease in every ornate bower,
Every moment an extended lifetime, yet life never fleeting seems,
Every flower shares its fragrance to the many hued denizen's dreams,
Its fiery colors with burning flame the butterfly to each flower spreads,
With refined delight smiles every flower where the butterfly steadily treads,
O reliever of sorrows , what joyous song of nature do you sing,
What messages of hope and freedom to humankind do you bring ?

10. Beyond the Wall

A low wall stands between this window and the world,
Of bare bricks, yet old and mosses cover the upper part,
When I open the window, I see the tall green grass
And the trees beyond , date palms dispersed in stately
abandon,
Others, standing in silence, displaying their greenery to the
morning clouds,
Grazing cows travel in slow steps, buffaloes trudge the path
with hogs,
Dogs are quiet in the morning, they have been active all night
Fighting territorial.battles with constant barking,
Shattering the tranquility of the night.;

Beyond the wall is a world , restless , yet imbued
With such mute beauty, green and tall,
There, butterflies fly with cheerful haste and cranes walk
Elegantly alongside cows in symbiotic existence;
The village lies ahead, where cattle roam with freedom ,
Women gossip, when the menfolk are away on the farm,
Their elders rest and, with keen eyes watch
The days pass by and time moving ominously on,
Children play bare feet and scantily clothed,

With smiles that fill their innocent countenances ;

A crow repeats its favorite syllable perched on a tree,
The banana tree spreads its large sheltering leaves,
The monsoon rains fall , freshening the greenery
With unsurpassed beauty, even the clouds enjoy
The scenic thrill, and with smiling shapes
Sail the majestic blue sky to far away lands;

Beyond the wall is a world,
Which heaven brings to the eager heart.

11. The Clouds

Like laced white ribbons in the azure sky
Vagrant clouds in abandon sail majestically by;
Brilliant sunlight shines amid traveling canopies of white,
With a rosy glow the color spreads , guided by infinite light;
From the earthly plain, dreams awake and above soar,
Riding the rays of the setting sun, they travel to heaven's door;
Messengers of peace , of empathy and devoted love,
Puffs of magic in the vast blue expanse above ;
Floating, fluttering , pushed by the wind and perennial dreams,
Forever they flow, undying, travelling to where the sun beam gleams .

12. Life like a candle

A candle spreads around its shining light,
Its flame dancing and flickering through the night,
Life like a candle, burns steadily away,
Spreading light from its heart till its dying day.

13. A little bud in bloom

Past rugged streets, past foreboding alleys of wanted care,
I came across a magnificent and well laid garden and there
I chanced upon a little bud in anticipated bloom,
When I walked with life's ordeals full of pending gloom;
The little bud offered the sight of pleasing and future delight,
Splendidly nurtured by nature , nourished by the day's light ;
Clouds had begun to gather above, ominous as the prevailing
sorrows of the day,
The rains were imminent, set to wash all grief in the heart
away,
Allaying all pain, sadness and life's gathered fears,
With hopes of a freshened morn would bring torrents of tears,
And soon the bud shall bloom into a gorgeous flower,
A new order would arrive, life shall evolve anew after the
celestial shower.

14. The Cyclone

The howling winds rushed through portals in the sky
In destructive fury, then descended upon the firmament ,
Waves, tossed up by a force from the bowels of the sea
Onward flowed , rising high with tumultuous power ,
Lashing on the shore with qualified rage,
Thunder roared through the dark clouds
As flashes of lightning gleamed like forked weapons ,
Trees waved in maddening sways
Till the water inundated the land
Wrecking homes , unleashing its wrath
With life at its mercy ,helpless cries drowned
By the deafening roar of divine strength ,
The might of the gods raged through the day
And beyond , leaving a trail of demolition ,
Till the heavens finally calmed and the powers above
Mercifully felt the crushing of humankind's vanity.

15. Where Heaven meets the Earth

I asked the traveler, "Where have you been?"
With a smile, he replied, " To where the vision of heaven I have seen,
Where clouds descend on the water and sand in divine mirth,
Where beauty and peace reigns, where heaven meets the earth."

16. The Aquarium

Streamlined figures of various colors and shapes seen,
Swimming in the water, shining in the light,
Passing, then darting behind stones and green,
A heart warming image in the dark night;

The little fish and the larger, in playful mirth,
A small home, the aquarium, waters little deep,
With unending joy the fishes swim from birth
Their abode secure these denizens keep;

The little boy with wondrous eyes does stare
At the world colored and with beauty laid,
The fish see the world outside so wonderful and fair,
Yet kingdoms apart, each do not the other's world pervade .

17. Humanity

Humanity soars, transcends time and space ,
The walls of religion, society's dismal face ,
Humanity unites, beyond caste and creed ,
Beyond color, hate and rampant greed ,
Humanity binds, with kindness and love
Peace spreads, with the message of the dove .

18. Arohee (one who ascends)

With a sweet, smiling countenance sat little Aarohee,
Placing a finger on her cheeks, she, aged only three,
Draped in a little sari her mother had made her wear,
She sat in contemplative thought, yet smiling with care,
With ornaments around and decorating her little head ,
She sat, with her little hands on the side of the bed;
Aarohee is the bright radiance in her home, reigning supreme,
She is the her parents', grandparents' and others' pride and dream,
Lights of the future sparkle in her candid and wide eyes,
Intelligence and curiosity makes her intelligent and somewhat wise,
She learns at a fast pace and evolves with care,
She knows the alphabets and talks fluent and fair ,
She can count objects from one to ten
And can write some alphabets with her little dot pen,
In two languages , she recites poems, her pronunciation strong and sound,
From "Twinkle Twinkle Little Star" to "The Wheels of the Bus go Round and Round",
She can sing the " Happy Birthday to You " song
In perfect melody, repeating every word from two verses long,

Aarohee knows and uses her mobile phone well,

Watching her favorite programs , her eager eyes can tell,

She prays in the Puja room with her mother along

And can even sing a few lines of a devotional song,

In the evening , with her father , she plays hide and peep,

She entertains her parents with many baby stories till they all

fall asleep,

Usually she plays with her little teddy bear,

And scolds him with little words when he doesn't care,

The little child is the future, as her life shall evolve,

She , with others,someday, shall perhaps society's and the

nation's problems solve;

There she sits, pretty, in her beautiful dress,

With glitters in her eyes, Aarohee, the little princess.

19. The Tanga (horse carriage)

The Tanga races through rugged streets , down history's lanes,
Its wheels roll with time's honored past in summer , winter
and drenching rains ,
The driver holds the reins as the horse moves with clattering
hooves,
As the carriage passes crowds and people gazing from roofs,
The past with a vision, once a glory ride,
With a nawab or a landlord with attendants inside,
Travelling to mansions where rose water and fountains play
To melodious music , rhythms of dance, which the mind
carries away ,
Under a festooned and embroidered canopy, people seated in
lavish seats ,
The swaying of the Tanga reverberated with the horse's hoof
beats;
Today the Tanga , with time worn canopy and seats,
Travels the same roads of old and the same journey repeats ,
Street urchins race behind , shouting with mischief and joy,
As the Tanga's wheels roll, the past reappears, scenes none can
destroy ,
Every horse of every Tanga gallops on the streets as their
ancestors had done in the past,

On the streets of Delhi, Lucknow, Rajgir , Jaipur and Burhanpur, the past shall always last,
Our forgotten heritages travel and reside on our ancient streets
In reveried silence , pulsating with the glories of old heartbeats.

20. The Heart

The heart beats with the power of love,
Of waves of compassion,mercy and more,
Rhythms of the heart sail to the skies above,
And travel with the clouds to heaven's door;
True human love is selfless and pure,
Of parents, siblings and friends, lofty and sublime,
Unending love for a beloved shall endure
Forever, the woes of life and the test of time,
The true heart knows the loss of the near and dear,
Every turmoil and joy it shelters within,
The brave heart travels with courage and without fear,
Life's every vagary the heart with strength shall endure therein.

21. The Swan

The swan sails over the silent lake
In quiet rhythm , not a ruffle does its wings make ,
Plumes as snow, white and pure,
Its blessed sight any sore eyes can cure;

The art of nature's skillful hand,
Whether on the water , whether on land,
In self propelled abandon, dispenser of joy and peace,
Pleasures of the heart, the swan's eulogies may never cease;

The wings of the swan reflect the dawn's golden sun ,
With noble waves the swan's day has begun,
There, in twilight, the swan can still be seen,
Swimming in freedom, heaven and earth in between ;

Under the starlit sky, clad in pristine white,
The swan is nature's marvel and delight,
As changing seasons pass, and when a new season is born,
The attire for eternal peace, by the swan is always worn .

22. Where the Heart is

I asked the traveler, "Where is your home?"
With a smile, he replied , "I reside where I roam,
Where my heart stays , there is where I live ,
To the earth and its people, my heart is all I can give ."

23. The village road

As I walked along the village road,
Past ploughed fields and shady green,
My hopes and heart above soared
When I saw the smile of a child so lean;

In her hands was a little branch of a tree
To guide the goats to their shelter and home ,
From the fields where the buffaloes graze free,
And the little goats with their mothers roam;

Barefoot she ran with her little brother beside ,
As gossiping women on the roadside sat,
The little boy with his eyes so wide,
Saw the world in a haze somewhat;

Children joined and ran along,
She smiled her carefree , shining smile,
The goats pranced, as if dancing to a song,
The village elders gazed all the while;

Far from the mansioned rich she lives and plays,
In rustic lands where sunshine is free,
Her shabby dress is rich in life always ,

Her village the abode of freedom be;

O village road , lead me there
Where humans share with creatures all ,
Poverty melts in the heart so fair;
And blessings of Nature arrive at every call.

24. Dreams

Strands of clouds hovering over the expansive blue,
Fragmented dreams, floating over a lost realm
Like derelict ships
Laden with treasures of mortal humans
Sans pilot , perennial peripatetics,
Who would dare to reach- who would dare
To bring them to Earth
Only to collide with reality's harshness?

25. Sleep

The night has its charms , when the eyelids close in restful sleep,
The mind travels to distant realms , parallel worlds, in space so deep ,
Travels in time , the mind's sojourn to the past, present and future seem
A matter of moments , yet unfolding periods would eternal deem.

26. The essence of life

Life that flows through veins of ours ,
Flows too in every blade of grass,
Life blooms in all fragrant flowers,
And every creature that comes to pass;
The rhythms of life beat in every tree,
Life radiates from each ray of the sun,
Full of life every little bacteria be,
All life on earth is unified in one;
Life is a mirror , the spirit its grace ,
Life is vibrant ,and living is its goal ,
The beauty of the mind does life embrace,
The essence of life is the eternal soul.

27. The Lotus

In murky waters, dispelling the gloom,
The lotus rises in splendor to bloom,
Radiant light of Nature on Earth,
To the Vision of beauty, it fosters birth;

Symbol of rebirth and purity sublime,
Spiritual enlightenment , transcending time,
The lotus engenders fresh beginnings anew,
As from the muddy swamp it shining grew;

From a gigantic lotus the sun was born,
Emerging from primeval waters, on a golden morn,
At every step of Buddha arose a lotus fine,
Seated atop the lotus does Lakshmi and Buddha shine;

In ancient Egypt the lotus would bring the dead back to life,
In the mythology of Greece tales of lotus-eaters are rife,
Connected to Vishnu, on the petals of the lotus , was Brahma born,
On pristine Earth, the lotus resided in the Primal Dawn

O lotus, eternal flower , spiritual and pure,
Blessed on Earth, your divinity shall forever endure .

28. War and Peace

Every war that mankind has ever fought,
Has seldom solved the problems it has earnestly sought,
Jingoism , ego, intolerance have caused unending grief,
Full scale wars have never been brief,
Peace eludes the populace when leaders for war strive ,
The people's hearts wait for the day peace shall arrive,
Every farmer and common people peace solely desire,
Many in vain in their sacrifice for peace never tire,
Empires may rise, empires may fall ,
Selfless love conquers one and all.

29. Mother Ganges

High in the mountains, fed from snow,
The Bhagirathi from a glacier begins its flow ,
From Gomukh to Gangotri in frenzied speed
To many branches, the river does lead ,
.As if Mahadev unlocked his holy hair,
And the Bhagirathi has settled there;

Thence downstream the turbulent waters
pass,
As a few tributaries join its gurgling course ,
Till at Devprayag its fast travelling mass
Meets the other headstream ,the Alakananda , away from its
source ;

Now at this confluence the Ganges does rise,
And descend downwards towards the plains,
The mother of all rivers, the home of the wise ,
Bountiful in her gifts, fed by the monsoon rains;

To Haridwar she travels , where on her hallowed shore
The Aarti every evening is a ceremony of light,
Lighted lamps are set sail as in days of yore
And blooming bells toll in unison every night;

In Allahabad , ancient Prayag three rivers meet,
The Kumbh Mela brings millions every twelve years ,
There the Ganges ,Yamuna and the elusive Saraswati greet,
And humankind is cleansed of all sins and fears;

And onto Varanasi the Ganges flows ,
The holiest of cities , founded by Shiva the Divine,
The most ancient city , Mother Ganges knows,
With temples and ghats, and the Aarti so fine ;

Past villages and towns, furrowed fields, trees and grass,
The river in silence moves along ,
Ages have passed and ages shall pass
All history is written in her waters' song;

As Patna , ancient Pataliputra , comes into view,
Great empires that rose and fell do memories bring ,
The Mauryas, The Guptas , have faded as the dew,
And the past has flown as a bird on its wing;

And thence the mother to Bengal arrives,
The final journey shall commence soon ,
Murshidabad , and then Kolkata , the City that thrives ,
The Hooghly bearing the waters of the Ganges with a boon ;

Past Kalighat , the abode of Kali , she reverently streams,

Below the Howrah Bridge lighted in colors at night,
Centuries of glory on her banks glowingly gleams,
The blue sky above a heavenly sight ;

Till last for the open sea she does head
At Sagar island her holy journey ends ,
Where Bhagirath brought back his brothers from the dead,
And with sacrifice and toil made amends;

Her other arm of water from Murshidabad goes
To Bangladesh where they call her Padma by name,
And with the Meghna she joins and flows
And mingles with the sea all the same;

Mother Ganges , you are the nourisher of humankind,
Your holy waters purify all creatures on earth,
You are the pacifier of the human mind,
Your blessings for all are forever worth.

30. Snow on the Mountains

As white fluffy cotton on the serene mountainside,

Snow glistening with golden sunshine on the mountains abide,

Carpeted in white, tranquil and pure,

The mountains at dawn , may eternal magic endure,

Echoes of the heart reflect on the pristine snow ,

And reverberate over the mountains where the morning sunlight shall grow,

Till twilight the snows smile, all the while glistening ,

With the chill wind and solemn air steadfastly listening ,

Stars twinkle over the white blanket at night,

The silhouetted mountains with snowflakes an empyrean sight,

When dawn breaks , and ray's strike the

snow in gold,

The view is eternal, for ages untold .

31. Dew on a leaf

Transient dew on a leaf, crystal clear,
A drop, a reflection of the world so near;
Reality's mirror , nature's crystal ball ,
O dewdrop, you reveal the mysteries of the world for all.

32. The footsteps of eternity

The sun sets and awakens the Eternal Mind ,
The silhouette of life, does in the reflected waters rest,
Footsteps of eternity does in every moment find
The touch of perfection, blessed at nature's behest .

33. The Festival of Kites

When the sun begins its journey north
And winter winds do severely bite,
To bask in the sun people come forth,
Young and old each fly a kite;

Swarming in the air of colors vast,
Floating and climbing with a twisting tail,
The kites outpace the birds so fast ,
In elegant harmony to the skies they sail;

The gods are appeased as the sun warmth brings,
Black is the color to wear for the day,
Children rum, pulling the kites' strings,
Happiness reigns, all are set in mirth and play;

From the mists of time, the festival was born,
Together with the first harvests reaped along,
As the kites fly in number and the skies adorn,
The Festival of Kites sings an eternal song.

34. Muse of the Night

Silently do you tread, in the moonlit night ,
Your soft footsteps shining in the light ,
Flowers strewn on the grass the dewdrops adorn ,
Muse of the night , you disappear with the early morn .

35. Song of the New Year

Farewell to the Old Year with saddened song,
As tides of greetings the New Year brings,
With blessings of happiness and peace along,
A symphony of joy the Divine Chorus sings;

The ethereal dove shall eternal peace bring,
In every heart shall sorrows end,
Every bird shall a greeting to the New Year sing,
Heaven on earth shall forever descend.

36. Twilight

Twilight, as the golden orb does descend
Towards the distant horizon and below,
Shadows of darkness shall transcend
The stars, and set silver moonlight aglow;

As the tree lined landscape fades from sight
And majestic silence reigns supreme,
Fireflies appear, clad in garments bright,
Shadowy boats sail the river to the land of dream;

Incessant chirps of crickets , the lonely bark of a dog,
A baby's distant cry, in its mother's arms,
Cattle returning home , through the evening fog,
The cool breeze flowing through the quiet farms;

In reverence to the conflux of night and day,
When life and time stand solemnly still,
The earth and sky whisper away,
And twilight gleams on the distant hill.

37. Fragrance

Over the wind has the fragrance spread ,
And over the soft , moist flowery bed ;
The Muse has left her footprints in the sand,
Love's footprints the sea leaves on enraptured land.

38. Freedom

Rejoice, for the bird that sings has flown
From its secluded cage and thrown
Freedom to the world, amidst the chains
Of life, and obliterated the accruing pains.

39. The Universe

The universe with its domain spread so vast ,
Galaxies , stars and planets of limitless number,
Nebulae , quasars , neutron stars and black holes that for ages last,
Connecting gas structures as neurons , all spurring with activity and no slumber;

Thirteen billion years ago perhaps it was born
With a bang so big and heat so large,
In that moment of birth at the earliest dawn
Were sown the seeds of its expansion and surge;

Generations of stars would gradually evolve ,
Solar systems and planets would acquire more elements with time ,
Conditions of order and complex life would unwritten equations solve,
Sentient beings would bring civilizations in suitable clime;

Advanced intelligence would the galaxies explore,
And colonies and homes build light years away,
They would harness the energies as never before
And to other universes through black holes find their way;

The structure of the universe does strangely seem ,
To be so similar to the neuron connected human brain,
The vast network part of an intelligence we deem ,
That regulates the laws and function of the entire demesne.

40. The Road to Chouparan

From the window of the van and its windscreen in front
Emerged the view of the road and surrounding green,
Winding and traveling to favorite haunts, I learnt,
Through villages and farms with scenic views seldom seen;

The road to Chouparan, through meadows and woods ,
Through three districts does it pass with pride,
Few vehicles in the morning [8]pass filled with goods,
Trees and cattle in silence together abide.

Houses of bricks and mud side by side,
Cattle stroll casually along the road,
At every turn of the rustic ride,
I see ponds and greenery and the humble peasants' abode;

At a certain turn, a scrap iron plant looms,
And then, women harvesting paddy on the fields,
At some crossing a pretty flower on a plant blooms,
The scene to the farmers working on the plough yields;

The woods around are a majestic, silent thrill,
Grass in the meadows sway with silent grace,

The air flows with such purity and will,
The steady breeze quietly caresses the face;

As raindrops fall on the viewing shield of glass,
The greenery fresher and greener seem,
Drenched cows without the need of an umbrella pass,
The falling dops in earnest the heart does redeem;

The road to Chouparan dwells amidst a rustic world,
A panorama of scenic life in vision does unfold,
Flashes of pensive thought sail with wings unfurled ,
The heart seeks fantastic realms of gold.

41. The Maidservant

Adversity written on her countenance , the maidservant
Rushes from household to household,
Performing her chores in dutiful fashion ,
Cleansing utensils , some rooms and occasionally some
cooking;
From early morn to evening her day is one
Of toil and rush , as her young son stays at home
With a father who does not work,
Who also makes regular visits to the liquor shop;

Her eldest son left about five years ago
And has not returned home since;
Another son worked in a different state
And has decided to return and live close to her ,
Eager to get him married , she has visited
Homes of a few prospective brides in the near villages,
The registration process over , she now waits
For the marriage on the fill moon day before the Holi Festival,
The bride could help with household work, she feels,
As she dreams of a brighter future ;

The maidservant brings local gossip to the homes
And tells of her family conditions to any listener,

The government offices provide her with rice and pulses
Every month, and the cash she earns
Maintains her family of non working males ;
In her eyes are visions of a personal home,
Built on a few acres of land she owns;
She works and walks with the dreams
Of a future better and prospective;
She reminisces with wide eyes as she cleans the floors .

42. The Lost City

Beneath the waves of the Khambat Bay,
Lies an ancient city ,gloried and ineffable. in its day,
Built by Krishna , the King Divine ,
With palaces of silver and crystals fine,
Encrusted with emeralds , shining light ,
The city of dreams , glittering in the night;
Boulevards, roads and markets so grand,
As if created by his magic wand ,
Houses and temples , as the gods decree,
The citizens lived, merry and free;
Ships from nations , far and near,
Traded at Dwarka, a port so dear ,
Majestic in size, elegance and grace
A city as such existed never before on the planet's face ;
The Mahabharata, Harivamsa and the Puranas of old,
Laud the fabled city , clad in gold,
Built by Vishwakarma on a single day,
Vying with Indra's city in heaven, all would say;
Fortified by walls with gates as grand as can be,
Palaces and mansions , as far as the eye could see;
Lines of houses , buildings so high ,
The upper storey would touch the sky;

Krishna's palace , built with skill divine, Coral pillars , inlaid
gems and sapphires so fine,
Seats and beds of ivory , set with gems alight,
Canopies of hanging pearls, the floors a heavenly sight ,
Fragrant incense , and peacocks so loud ,
Who believed the aroma issued from a cloud;
Such magnificence beheld Dwarabati, the city of dream,
Where life and time would eternal seem ;
Yet the days after Krishna's demise,
One inauspicious hour, the sea would rise,
And inundate the city, palace and all beside,
The beautiful city, would below the waves reside;
O Dwarka! In people's vision you shall again rise ,
As archaeologists discover your ruins and surmise,
There once was a city, the grandest of all,
That sank beneath the sea ,but would emerge again
At humankind's call .

43. On the conjunction of Jupiter and Saturn

Four centuries have passed since the great gods met,
In the vast realm of hallowed space,
Jupiter, benefactor of health, wealth and jovial set,
Saturn , strict and disciplined in blessed grace;

When all other gods from the heavens watch ,
As nearer the Titans align with sacred Earth
A new star blazes in the sky alike a torch
And shines tonight for all of divinity's worth;

What blessings do the tidings bring,
To the teeming multitudes of humankind,
What eternal song does the universe sing,
In joyous harmony , enlightening the mind.

44. The pensive bird

A solitary bird, in pensive mood,
Perched atop a mound it steadfastly stood,
What earthly problem did it ponder on?
Fleeting bird, now here and then gone.

45. Sailing Ship

Sail away My friend, on life's sailing ship,
No farewells will be said on this parched lip
Till the liquor enlivens the thirsty heart -
Then, turning to life's woes, let's watch them depart.

46. Love's demure eyes

I drank from the cup at your behest ,
My fears such as these may be laid to rest,
While love's demure eyes to the earth did gaze,
The seas did part and the skies did amaze .

47. The tranquil night

The words of silence, in the tranquil night ,
Showered by the moon's serene light ,
Spreads to the stars, in serried grace,
Where dwells the image of an angelic face;
As the twinkling stars travel the sky ,
The night lingers, refusing to die ;
The dawn shall the memories of night bring ,
When flowers bloom and the birds sing ;
Throughout the night, these whispers of the heart,
Shall endure forever, and never depart .

48. Eternal Life

In our hearts breathes the Celestial Fire,
In our minds reigns the Universe,
The vastness of space do dreams inspire
And life for eternity does rehearse.

49. The Palm Tree

Standing as a sentinel, beside the rough road,

The palm tree , slender and tall, resides in its open abode;

Beneath the clouds and the pristine sky,

Few trees in the neighborhood, and a couple of dwellings nearby;

Tranquility reigns, save the occasional sound of a tractor and a car,

A few voices that sound as if from afar;

The country road towards the village does slowly wind,

An indelible impression, it overwhelms the wandering mind .

50. Wisdom

The drunken stupor that enables me to write
As the halls of knowledge my hands prepare to smite ;
Wisdom, let thy wings over the blue unfold,
And life in meaningful ways prepare me to mold.

51. The Festival of Light

Display of fireworks on the ground or in air,
Lamps and lights, festooned everywhere ,
The streets adorned , this colorful night
Shall families rejoice, on the Festival of Light,
Sweets and savories do all joyously share,
This night of belonging, the night of care;
When King Rama of Ayodhya to home returned,
All welcomed the victor, as myriads of lamps burned .

52. Goddess Durga

For ten days O Goddess, you visit
The land of mortals;
From your heavenly abode in Kailash
You travel with your offsprings
Each of whom are Gods and Goddesses ,
Kartik, Ganesh, Saraswati and Lakshmi
The lion, your devotee and Mount ;
You arrive at the auspicious hours and days
When humans rejoice with festivities
And devotions to you O Goddess
Durga;
Invincible mother, slayer of demons ,,
All encompassing Shakti in ineffable glory ,
Consort Of Shiva the Almighty;
Drums, bells and conch shells herald your arrival
With fervent prayers of hope
As you usher peace and safety
To innumerable and frail humans ,;
Your nine forms and names have
Battled the demon Mahisashur for ten days
Armed with the weapons of the Divine forces
Each in your ten hands, neither God not mortal ,
You are the power born fully grown

Dispelling the forces of evil ,
The ultimate deliverance for humankind ;
When you depart every year on the tenth day
Mortals weep and await your arrival
In the following year to their world.

53. The path to the woods so green

The path that leads to the woods so green
Where leaves rustle and trees are serene,
Light emerges in rays so fine,
The wandering mind meets the heart of mine;
The cow grazes since the rain
Walking alongside a friendly crane,
The birds fly with their companions along, Settling on the
branches with full throated song ;
The fallen leaves I trample with care,
The wild flowers do in amazement stare ;

A little journey, A timeless seek
Into a realm where nature shall fondly speak.